FORWARD

Russ Steimle has captured the essence of what it takes to organize a group of diverse international people into teams that can get the job done.

Integrating and building high performing teams across geographies and cultures is a complex process, yet Russ boils it down to key pieces of profound wisdom using a simple and plain, yet powerful writing style.

Through years of personal experience in the front line he acquired and tested the key pieces of knowledge required to build international high performing teams. The sales and support teams he has built in both Europe and Latin America is a testament and a legacy to the value of this wisdom!

This book reminded me what da Vinci once said: "simplicity is the ultimate sophistication". Well done Russ!

Edmundo Muniz, MD, PhD, MSc

PREFACE

I have been team building for over 25 years. I have learned that without a strong, enthusiastic, and competent team it is very difficult to achieve business objectives. The sooner we as business leaders realize this, the sooner we will attain the desired results.

My sales and support teams have been mainly in the international arena. First in Europe, and currently in Latin America. They have consisted of direct employees, dealers, representatives and agents. Looking on my team building experience, I recognize that the endeavor has been, not only successful, but enjoyable and rewarding. It reminds me of the saying, *"if you do something that you love to do, you will never work a day in your life."*

I had not thought too much about my team building skills until recently when a close friend, Pedro (who was a member of one of my teams in the past) complimented me, "Russ, You are the best team builder I know; You have a gift, tell me how you do it, so I can build my team."

 I was appreciative of his heart-felt praise, thanked him, and told him the honest truth, as I saw it. "It's just Stupid Simple." Maybe I had just coined a new adjective to

describe team-building, I don't know, but it did put me to think.

What I consider to be a *"stupid simple"* concept, is what comes to me naturally and without a great deal of effort, but it is fundamental to building a successful business. So I decided to share what made me a successful team builder not just with Pedro, but with all business leaders who wanted to listen.

What I will share with you is actually a compilation of life events, examples of others, and ideas that I have applied to my life and work situations with surprising success. I love people, and I get great satisfaction in seeing others succeed and accomplish their dreams and objectives.

There is powerful and positive energy that is experienced when a team accomplishes the goal that its members set out to do. It is this energy that keeps the group motivated to continue setting higher and higher goals, then go and achieve them.

I felt the same kind of high energy the first time I went to a soccer match in a stadium in Sao Paulo, Brazil. It was palpable; I actually felt it flow through my body. It's the energy that drives the soccer teams to play harder, and score goals. That is the energy that I love to build within my teams.

Here are my thoughts, tips and some of what I consider to be secrets, to successful international team building. Who knows, maybe you too would say at the end, *"that's stupid simple"*.

CONTENTS

CHAPTER 1. – STUPID SIMPLE

CHAPTER 2. – THE BODY ANALOGY

CHAPTER 3. – INTERNATIONAL ENVIRONMENT

CHAPTER 4. – INT'L TEAM BUILDING ESSENTIALS

- High Energy
- Thankfulness
- Recognition
- Getting to know the team
- Be nice, but not too nice
- Communication
- Meetings
- "Outside" Members
- Food
- Everyone is Important
- Honesty
- Positive outlook
- Language barriers
- Concept of time

CHAPTER 5. – A RECAP

CHAPTER 1. – STUPID SIMPLE

 What is "stupid simple" for one person may not be for another. But the good thing is that it could become that, if you want it bad enough. I believe that anyone can do anything they want to; it all depends on how badly they want it.

How much work are you willing to put into something in order to be good at it, or maybe even the best at it? Everyone came to the planet with a gift or a propensity for being successful at something. The fact that one has a gift however does not mean that no work is involved, it means that if you put in the work, you will achieve your goal and enjoy the process.

Everything we do has an element of learning associated with it. That is the case with athletes, artists, scientists, teachers, or any other profession. In the case of elite athletes, we see the results every four years during the Olympics, but we were not there to observe the long hours of practice, the falls, the injuries, the disappointments. So we think, *"They're just good at it."* They make that sport look *"stupid simple,"* and that in itself is a talent.

Teachers are another example of gifted professionals who put in an extraordinary amount of work, time, and effort to excel in their field. They have passion and creativity, yes; some also have a *gift* for teaching that makes what they do seem seamless and effortless.

It appears to be second nature for some teachers to identify students' needs and come up with the key that opens the door for them to succeed. These are also the teachers and classrooms that students remember for the rest of their lives.

At one point in their life these exceptional teachers made it their mission and goal to use their natural abilities to be the best. They would probably say that teaching is *"stupid simple."*

The fact that you're reading this little book means that you're probably somehow involved in team building, so you might have a predisposition, a desire, maybe even (like me) a passion for this art. You just need hard work, practice and pointers from others to help you build your team-building muscles. But because you have a gift in this area, and a desire to be better at it, you will enjoy the experience also.

Team building for me is *"stupid simple,"* because I enjoy it and get great pleasure in seeing the financial and personal results achieved from a team that is driven to accomplish great things.

On the other hand, there have been some things that I've had to learn that were nowhere near the "Stupid Simple" spectrum, but that with a lot of work, and more than a little amount of frustration, eventually made it to that "stupid simple list." Read on.

My job took me to live in Sao Paulo, Brazil for a while, which is one of the largest cities in the world – over 20 million people. Getting around in Sao Paulo can be frustrating to say the least. The heavy traffic and endless number of streets, none of which go in a straight line, filled with drivers who think they are on a race track, drove me to exasperation.

One of my friends born and raised in Sao Paulo, who had at one time been a taxi driver in the city told me that it was "simple" to get around. He went on to add that he *enjoyed* driving in Sao Paulo and finding new ways to get around the city; he even found "short cuts" to avoid traffic as much as possible, he alleged.

What my friend said made no sense to me, how could he say that it was simple? But I knew one thing for sure, if I was going to live and work in Sao Paulo, I had to find a way to get around the city, I wanted it really bad... then it happened, I saw her.

She looked to be about 80 years old, driving in the lane next to me in the middle of rush hour traffic, seemingly with not a care in the world. There were 12 lanes of traffic that were barely creeping along, and there were hundreds of motorcycles (*motoboys*) weaving between the stopped cars, like cockroaches scurrying when the lights go on. Ok I said, "If she can do this, I can too!"

My friend, the former cab driver, suggested that I buy the official Sao Paulo road guide, (this was in the days before GPS). I bought the 500-page guide of the city and studied it. Many times I found myself along the side of the road looking at the maps trying to figure out where I was, and which streets went where. After a few weeks I was able to navigate well through Sao Paulo, and even had figured out some "short cuts." Now I can almost be a tour guide of the streets of Sao Paulo Brazil, and I don't live there anymore.

In fact, some of my friends who have lived in Sao Paulo all their lives have told me that I know the city better than they do. With some more practice and time it could even become, "stupid simple."

Determining to excel at something is the first step in having what you do become "stupid simple". The second step is realizing that everyone is capable of learning how to achieve their objectives if they want it bad enough.

There are some basic fundamentals in team building to learn, that when put into practice will reward you with an enthusiastic and results-driven team, no matter how diverse your team is, and you can be on your way to making team building *"stupid simple."*

CHAPTER 2. – THE BODY ANALOGY

Our bodies are a metaphor for how a team works together to accomplish goals. We have a head, hands, feet, toes, fingers, eyes, and internal organs that all work together to help us go where we want to go, and do what we want to do. Our bodies do it all so effortlessly that it's easy to take this incredible machine for granted.

As I am sure you have figure out, the head is the leader. It comes up with great ideas and thinks about how to implement them. But the head can only sit there looking good, and full of ideas; it might roll around a bit, but it won't go anywhere without the rest of the body parts, or team members, to help it.

Without a neck to swivel the head around, the eyes in our head can only see in one direction. Our ears are able to hear, but cannot determine where the sound is coming from.

Without arms, hands and fingers we would have a difficult time to get nourishment to our mouths. (If we were Italian, without hands we couldn't even speak).

Without legs, feet and toes, we couldn't move the body in the direction that we need, or would like it to go.

Without a strong heart, we couldn't pump the nourishment to the other body parts, or team members, to keep them functioning.

Another crucial point is that if the head does not have clear thoughts and purpose to direct the body, the individual parts would all wander all over the place and go in their own direction, but without getting anywhere. The head pulls the team together and keeps the members focused.

Our bodies are the ideal example of how a team works in harmony, with each part doing what it's designed to do, in order to move effortlessly and efficiently in the direction that it needs to go.

From the first day of life, our body parts begin to learn what their jobs are. When we begin to walk our legs wobble and shake, but with practice, we soon we are off and running. Our arms guide our hands to put whatever they find in our mouth, until the head instructs the hands that the main function of the mouth is to ingest *nourishment* into our body, and not just anything that the hand places in it.

 This body analogy became even clearer to me one day, during my daily ritual of bike riding: I like to follow the same route on my 15km trek, always keeping track of how much time it takes me while constantly trying to shave off a few minutes or seconds of time.

In my head, I determine what route to take and I assess the surroundings (weather, wind, temperature, etc.) before I make the decision to start out on the trip. I know that my goal is to beat my last time, and I make improvements, where needed, to achieve my goal.

I need my legs to keep driving my feet to push on the pedals in a systematic forward pattern in order to make the bike move forward. If they would push on the pedals backward, I would be unable to move. My legs automatically know what to do, I don't have to tell them each time what their task is. I had taught them many years ago when I first learned to ride a bike and now this knowledge kicks in automatically every time I get on my bike. The body parts do great team work, without my continuous input, or worry about their performance.

All the while that I am moving forward, the eyes in my *head* are watching the road to avoid obstacles or potential problem areas. When necessary, my arms turn the bike to keep it on the correct path. My shoulders help to keep me balanced and my fingers keep poised to engage the brakes when needed.

As I continue to ride further and faster, my heart rate increases to move more nutrients to the other members of my body, and my lungs process more oxygen to feed the blood.

The amazing thing about this *team* is that as long as I do my part planning the course, and watching where we are going, all of the members do what they're created and trained to do. And the longer we work together, the better they get at their job.

This analogy doesn't stop here. As the *head* of this bike riding team *(body)*, it is essential that I supply the necessary tools to ensure that the entire *team* functions at optimal capacity. Always keeping in mind the goal of improving the riding time.

The bike needs to be in top working order: The tires have to be properly inflated, the brakes and gears well oiled. If possible, it's best to have a top quality bike, which would deliver the best times with the least amount of effort. At times, however, *budget constraints* prevent me from getting a high quality bike, in which case I need to perform the best I can, with what I have.

In search of attaining the best possible riding time, I downloaded a bike riding app for my iPhone. It tracks my route, gives me the average speed that I ride at, and the time that it takes me to complete my desired route. This information allows me to adjust my body (the team) until it achieves the desired outcome.

I might have to consider bringing in some "outside" team members to help me gain some time on achieving my goal. More on "outside" team members later, but for now I will tell you that I did bring in a member that greatly affected the outcome of my riding time, without physically being attached to the team. This "outside" team member is the gate guard of the community that I live in.

His job is to check the ID, and register everyone that goes in and out of the community. Each time I left the community, I needed to sign out, and then sign back in on the return. Overall, the process added about a minute to my riding time. I decided to befriend the guard; I told him about my biking hobby and exchanged some other pleasantries.

After that, my newly-added team member simply waved me through the gate. I made a big leap in time reduction simply by involving the help of others to help me accomplish my goal.

Next comes one of the most important procedures when working with the bike riding *team*. Once I return, all sweaty and tired from a nice ride, I jump in the shower to reward my team with a nice warm, soothing, and refreshing wash-down to relax the muscles. If needed, I even rub a bit of ointment on my knees to make them feel better. It is my way of saying "thank you" to the team for helping me accomplish my goal another day, hopefully beating my last riding time. After the shower, we all enjoy a nice snack and usually a nice cold beer and reflect on the accomplishment reviewing the numbers provided by my neat iPhone app.

Sure most anyone can ride a bike and or do other activities like this, but to *realize* that it is a true well balanced team that has done this, takes more of an appreciation and awareness of the team and its abilities.   It's also knowing and understanding that without the team it would be neither possible, nor enjoyable to do. Team members need to know their importance, and realize that the head also recognizes it, by showing them the appreciation they deserve

CHAPTER 3. – INTERNATIONAL ENVIRONMENT

 My interest in the international milieu began when I was in high school and I decided to take an elective course in German language. That didn't start out very well, so my parents suggested that we get a foreign exchange student from Germany that would help me learn the language. It sounded like a good idea, and we started the process of getting our German exchange student. As it turned out, there were only exchange students available to host from South America. So we got one from Chile, and I quickly changed my elective to Spanish.

During that year, my Chilean brother and I became good friends and I learned a lot about other people's beliefs and cultures. I found it so fascinating that I decided to become an exchange student myself and between my junior and senior year of high school off I went to Santiago, Chile to live with the family of my Chilean brother.

It soon became clear to me that there was a big difference between learning about other countries and cultures from books or simply meeting someone from another country, and actually being immersed in a different culture by living in a foreign environment. It required *me* to adapt to the culture that I was living in.

I discovered new and different family relationships. In Chile, and as I later found out, in many other parts of the world, children lived at home with their parents a lot longer than they did in the US. Their focus was not in trying to get away from home, but rather on how they would succeed in the world, get an education, find a career, and better their lives.

Their social and political surroundings, as well as the culture that they were part of, had shaped them into the individuals that they were. These same factors influenced their philosophy about life, their religious beliefs, and their work ethic.

It didn't make them better or worse people than me, just different; and their circumstances caused them to view the world differently than the way I saw it, including the way they related to work.

It dawned on me that in this huge new world that I had come in contact with, most people had not experienced the type of life that I had grown up with in my small West Michigan town, and that, in turn, had shaped me into who I was.

I was brought up in a very religious environment that left little room for diversity of ideas, philosophies or even people. I was particularly struck by the inclusion that I felt in Chile, regardless of the fact that I was from a different country, a different culture, a different language, a different religion... this all seemed to have little or no importance.

I was privileged to discover this wonderful outside world at an early age, I found this experience enlightening and refreshing and it would be a deciding factor later on in my career choice.

After returning home to West Michigan, with a new and vastly expanded mind, I was very open to new opportunities now that I had developed an appreciation for the diversity that the world offered.

During my high school years my parents continued to host exchange students from other parts of the world, so by the end of my senior year, I had gained two additional brothers, Eduardo from Uruguay, and Krister from Sweden. I in turn passed this eye-opening opportunity on to my children and hosted a number of exchange students in our home as they grew up.

During my senior year of high school, I also met my future wife Tina, who just happened to be from the Dominican Republic. That sealed the deal! International was in my blood.

As I started my working life, I was fortunate to get a job as a Chemist for a world leading German chemical company. One of my colleagues was an expat that had been transferred to the US from the German headquarters. I liked this idea, now I had a new goal; *someday I would become an expat and work in another country.*

I set out to investigate the possibilities and kept the dream in the front of my mind. My positions within the company changed from chemist to customer support and I had various opportunities to travel to the company headquarters in Germany, but no expat positions opened up.

Some years later, while working for another company, my dream became a reality. I was in charge of working with a rep group in Paris, France, that sold our products. My company had made the decision to buy out this rep group and set up our own subsidiary in Paris. This new office would manage the sales and support of our products in France, Spain, and Italy.

One day while discussing how the transition would take place, my boss Joan, asked me if I would be interested in going to live in Paris for a year to help the transition go smoothly. I said that I would think it over. 30 seconds later I said yes. Joan told me that I should at least consult my wife first. I did, it helped that she had studied French in college and loved the French culture, so after some planning, my wife and I headed off to beautiful Paris.

I had traveled to visit the group in Paris on several occasions previously, and traveled to other locations in Europe, Asia and the Middle East as well. I even felt that I was quite an experienced international business man. But I soon realized that I still had a lot to learn about how other people lived, worked, and just how big of a role, culture plays in the decision making process.

When traveling back and forth to various international locations, most of us stay in hotels, eat in restaurants, ride in taxis, and for the most part, speak in English because everyone seems to speak enough to communicate. I was no different.

When we arrived in Paris, we found ourselves needing to learn how the public transportation system worked because taxis weren't going to be practical. Living in a hotel got old very quickly, so we began the process of apartment hunting; we immediately found out that we needed to buy all new appliances for the kitchen of the apartment, including the kitchen sink, because the kitchen in most apartments was just an empty space, without even the cupboards.

English was not as widely spoken as I had hoped, so I began the arduous task of learning enough French to help me communicate. I also needed to find a way to develop my own circle of local friends, since I didn't want to rely solely on the people that worked for me to take me around, and show me how things worked. In other words, I needed to adapt because France was not going to change for me. I needed to adapt to France, and that was the way it should be.

The experience itself made me realize that in order to accomplish my goals. I needed to fit in and learn how everyone else in France did things, rather than to expect them to do things my way. I needed to organize my own team, and I needed their help in reaching the business goals that the company expected.

So I enthusiastically began the process of organizing the business in a foreign country with many unfamiliar regulations. With my small group of newly-acquired team members, who came with the acquisition, I began to build my team.

I knew my goals, so first I needed to explain clearly to the team what these goals were. Besides the fact that we needed to grow sales and service, we also needed to develop brand awareness and customer awareness in the market.

I boldly informed my new team that I would be "in charge" of growing this business and together, as a team, we were going to get the job done. We would need to make some changes in the way things had been done in the past, because the new expected targets were much higher than they had previously been

Our first task was to examine what we needed to do to in order to grow the sales. After reviewing past years' results and sales figures, something caught my attention. It was evident to me that during the month of August there were always very low sales. When discussing this with the team I was informed that in

France it is traditional for everyone in the country to take their vacation in the month of August and there were never strong sales during that month.

Seeing this as my opportunity to show that I was in charge, and that now things would be different, I proceeded to inform my team that we would break with this tradition. From now on we would remain open for business during the month of August, as we did in The United States of America. Everyone in our team needed to figure out other times during the year to take their vacation.

After making my new proclamation they all said that it would be a great idea. But before I could break into a complete smile, I heard a *"however."* Followed by an important question, "to whom would we sell if everyone else, including all our customers, are on vacation during August?" Making appointments would be nearly impossible.

Additionally, they pointed out, when the team members did take their own vacations, during the other months of the year, it could be at a bad time for the company to be short on staff. Business was usually active and steady during the remaining months of the year.

I had just had my first rude awaking. Even though I was in charge and thought that I had a really good idea, I needed the input of the others in the team to make wise decisions.

The cultures and traditions of people play a big role in how the team performs. I was humbled, and from that point on decided that "being in charge" was not best done autocratically, but rather  by giving serious consideration to the input of all the team members in order to move forward, smoothly and efficiently.

From that moment on, we began to form a team that worked like a well-oiled machine. We were able to find some very good ways to grow the sales together. This team knew how to work hard together and play hard together. As a matter of fact that became our group motto: "Work hard, Play hard." We had business strategy meetings together, and went out and enjoyed social times together. There were times that we would start a business meeting at one of our favorite restaurant/bars at 5 pm and not realize it was time to go home until everyone in the place was gone after 3 am in the morning. In the culture that I was in, this is how you got results.

My French team, did all the work that they had signed up for, and all I needed to do was keep us all focused, facilitate the activities that kept them enthusiastic, and mentor them in the expectations of working for an American company.

Continual reporting to them on our status and direction was all it took to keep the team interested and excited about our business. The more I supported and empowered them, the more they supported me. I supported their ideas, cared about them as employees and as people. I praised them on their great work and shared with them the glory of achieving our goals.

I did not try to change them or their culture, but rather, tried to understand what was important to them and what made them want to be successful.

My original one-year term assignment, turned out to be five years, and expanded from being responsible for the regions of France, Italy and Spain, to include the entire area of north and south Europe. The area grew to include an office in the UK that covered Scandinavia and we created a new office in Italy.

CHAPTER 4. – INT'L TEAM BUILDING ESSENTIALS

I cover in this book, mainly International team building, because that is where my assignments have taken me. But most of these ideas and tips work well for building all types of teams. These fundamentals are global.

An important quality in a leader is genuineness. This requires transparency, which is probably one of the most difficult attributes to attain because it requires at least some degree of vulnerability. But without transparency, it is very challenging to build a team that can fully realize their potential and move in a synchronized way, since the members will find it difficult to open up and share their concerns.

The goal of the team leader is to keep the energy of all members moving in the same direction. The team as a whole needs to be focused on the tasks at hand, and aware of the progress that is being made.

When all of the energy of the group is pushing in the same direction, the load is lighter, the progress will be steady, and the goal will be obtained quicker, than if the group energy is scattered in various directions, or a team member is not focused on the right goal.

An autocratic type leader is one that needs everything to go his or her way, and usually results in the selfish desire of getting all the glory and recognition that comes with accomplishing a goal. These leaders would have a difficult time shaping a well- functioning and focused team.

Team members who are made to feel that there is nothing rewarding for them in the job, other than a paycheck, won't be interested, let alone enthusiastic, in helping to reach a goal. After all, they don't feel part of any team, just a tool for someone else to use.

This is most relevant to international teams, because many of the members have probably worked under an autocratic type of leader, at some point.

Additionally, chances are that in some international situations, the members of the team have actually lived under the rule of a political dictator.

They have seen the outcome of these situations and know that the "worker bees", hardly ever make out well. The subjects of dictators generally complain and look for ways to get out from under the dictator's rule. They plot, plan, dream, of ways to go in other directions; many often risk their lives in their pursuit of a life where their voice is heard.

In "Latin" cultures a *Macho* mentality is still alive and well. Latin company owners are sometimes seen as kings and rulers, supreme *jefes*. They may have a functional and even successful business, but they won't be accomplishing what they could if they operated as a team. Praise needs to be shared with the team, they're the ones that help leaders arrive where they want to go.

Constant micromanagement of team members is counterproductive. It disempowers the team members and it creates an environment of dependency that robs them of the creativity and initiative that are essential to get the work done.

Although control of overall direction is important, encouraging autonomy on the part of members of a team displays the ultimate form of appreciation, trust and gratitude. Sharing responsibility lightens the load and increases the output potential of the members.

They work harder and take more personal pride in the results.

High Energy

As a leader, one of our responsibilities is to maintain a high energy level in the work place. Enthusiasm is  actually contagious as we experienced in our French office. I mounted a fairly large bell near the entry door.   Each time one of the team members secured an order they went to the bell and rang it loudly so that all that were in the office knew we had received an order. When we heard the bell ring the whole team would shout out and congratulate the "ringer."   This was great, however, after a short time the bell was ringing so much and everyone was cheering so often, that we almost couldn't get our work done.

Thankfulness

Expressing gratitude is a key ingredient in building an effective team. My parents taught me at a young age to always say "Please and Thank you." These powerful words should be used often and freely with members of the team, even if what they do is a normal and an expected part of their job. It's good to find something specific to praise a team member. Maybe they accomplished a task on time, or neatly. Maybe they put in some extra time or they arrived early to a meeting, it's beneficial to let them know that everything they do as part of the team, is noticed and is important.

Recognition

Thanking and recognizing your team members' achievements in front of their peers contributes to camaraderie and cooperation among team members.

In my regular group review meetings with the team, I  make sure to point out at least one thing that each member has contributed to help the team reach the desired goals. Mentioning members by name creates a real feeling of ownership of the contribution that they have made.

There is a sense of pride that comes when a person is recognized for their accomplishments. No matter what position someone has in a company they will tell you that recognition feels good, so I always remember to pass this feeling on to others.

A small thing can have great rewards.

Getting to know the team

Taking time to get to know your team members, both professionally and personally is another contributor to the increase of productivity. Families are important to all of us, but it seems to take more of a central role in certain geographical areas, Latin America being one of them. Getting to know at least the immediate family of team members ensures that they will deliver their best. I insist that the members of my team make sufficient time in their schedules to be with their families  and do family activities. After all if spouses are happy, the members will be happy also, and happy members work harder.

I have attended birthday parties, weddings, graduations and family cook-outs. I have even been granted the honor of being godfather to the son of one of my team members. And my son's godfather is one of my former colleagues from France.

The more the team leader gets to know the members of the team, the more confidence and trust is developed between each other. Additionally, the leader gains insight into what areas are better suited for each member.

Be nice, but not too nice

One of my bosses once told me that it was okay to get close to and *"be nice"* to the members of the team, because that seemed to be working well for me, as he saw the great relationship that I had with my team members. "But don't be too nice," he added later on. What my boss was trying to teach me was to find a balance between being a nice boss, and using my leadership skills.

Sometimes as leaders we must make difficult decisions to increase efficiency and output. One of those difficult decisions is to release a team member from the team. My teams work well most of the time and I rarely have to dismiss members; but when it does happen, I remind the rest of the team of our goals and direction, which sometimes are better attained with changes in personnel.

I do admit to them that changes are not always pleasant, even for me, and I allow team members to deal with the changes in the manner that they see fit, as long as it doesn't affect the work flow and productivity of the rest of the members.

Communication

My international teams are mostly comprised of direct employees. But we also rely on reps, dealers and agents, to whom I bestow equal importance and appreciation. Why? Often, for them, my company represents only a part of their overall business, since they usually represent or sell products for other companies. Granting these reps and dealers recognition and a place in the team insures that they give priority to the sale of our products.

Appreciation and recognition come in the way of training, support, updates and corporate information.

 We include our reps and dealers in conference calls from the core team, and even corporate. They have access to the same communication tools as everyone else, in order that we can attend to their questions and concerns rapidly and efficiently.

Good communication channels are key when working with a team whose members are spread over a large geographical region. For instance, I realized that various members of my Latin American team held vast amounts of information that had not been shared with the rest of the team. It was not intentional, but rather a gap in our communication. Nevertheless, had everyone possessed the same information, it would have expedited many sales.

Our solution came in creating a *WhatsApp* group. We developed a rapid way for questions and information to be distributed throughout the group. All members had smart phones and all used *WhatsApp* for personal texting, so developing a "chat group" was a simple, and immediate solution to making sure that essential information, previously unavailable to all, was shared.

Sometimes I wonder how we ever did anything without smart phones, but I do not miss the days of fax machines. There are many technology tools available today that can make our tasks easier and better, and it's worthwhile to regularly evaluate and update your team's communication tools.

Meetings

Group meetings, especially a well-planned sales meeting is a venue to do several team building activities at once. This is valuable time for sharing useful information, personal interaction among team  members, and an opportunity for team members to interact with any "outside" members that the leader choses to bring to the meeting.

While working in France with my team I had the opportunity to organize a complete European sales meeting. We brought in the sales and support team members from all over Europe: my French team, the German team, the UK team.

I also made sure to invite many "outside" members comprised of corporate managers, engineers, product/marketing staff, and finance personnel.

All groups shared information, answered important questions and addressed concerns that otherwise would have taken unnecessary amounts of time to clarify. Besides the important day conferences where everyone gained an abundance of useful information, and hopefully insight, we planned recreational events in the evenings.

These entertaining events allowed the group to interact and get to know each other better in a friendly and relaxed environment.

One of our most fun events was a *"go-karting"* night. We arranged several racing teams which consisted of only one nationality or job type represented per team. At times we ended up with one German, one French, one Italian and one Spaniard in one team, or one engineer, one finance person and a sales person on another.

 It turned out to be an incredibly successful event where, at the end of the night, I actually saw the Germans hugging the French and  Italians, and the engineers high-fiving everyone. Huge

walls of indifferences and misunderstandings came tumbling down.

I have been able to repeat this type of meeting/event with other teams, always with similar results.

"Outside" Members

As previously mentioned, "outside" members of the team are essential. Just like the gate guard in my bike riding example, there are people that are indispensable to help the team succeed.

I have found that in international business, corporate members have little confidence in how the international sales team deals with finances and especially credit terms. Unfortunately, this lack of trust is at times warranted. That is why I made it a point to include John, the corporate controller from one of the companies that I worked for, to participate and be involved in the activities of my sales team. Not only in the activities directly related to work, but also in the social activities. This allowed John to have interaction with everyone in the team, including the agents, dealers and reps.

John was now able to put a face and personality with the international team members. He understood their responsibilities and appreciated being included in the team. According to John, the inclusion made his job more enjoyable and easier to do.

"Outside" Members are an asset to help move the team forward, and there are a lot of them that can be included. Be sure to make these valuable members feel as an integral part of the team, receiving the same respect that is given to the other members.

Food

Food is one of my "secrets" for building good relationships with my international teams. When I am with team members in their country I eat and enjoy their local foods. I have to admit that it was not difficult to eat the local foods in France, Italy and Spain, but no matter where you are you can encounter some very "interesting" dishes that

 wouldn't probably be part of your typical diet. Remember, food is like a religion in some cultures, it represents a lot more than

nourishment, it means *"you're my friend," "welcome," "I like you," "you're part of my family."*

One of my celebrity heroes is Anthony Bourdain. His TV show is about getting to know how people really live in other countries around the world. He mainly sits around the table and eats whatever meals and drinks, the local people prepare for him. During mealtime, he finds out about people's cultures and their personal lives. He takes his viewers to places, and introduces them to people that the average tourist will never have the opportunity to meet.

Bourdain said on one of his shows that if everyone ate more meals together, there would be a lot less troubles in the world. I agree. It is one of the doors to people's hearts.

Something as small as sharing a local meal with someone really means a lot to them and says, I accept you.

Everyone is Important

Treating others the way you would like to be treated, or practicing the *Golden rule* towards *all* members of the team, contributes to high performance. Some team members might go unnoticed, but that does not diminish their importance. It's like the toes of your feet, they don't make themselves known very often; in fact we keep them covered most of the time, but when they have an in-grown toe nail the pain can affect the whole body, and it slows down the process of getting around.

I remember working with Scott, a great salesman that recognized the importance of everyone in a company.

 When we visited customers, Scott greeted everyone, the receptionist, the janitor, the lab workers... with a smile, kind words, a firm handshake, small talk and even inquired about their families.

I quickly noticed the special treatment that he received from everyone in the company, and the excellent service that they gave him. Scott never had a problem securing an appointment to visit the company and never had to wait long to be received by the clients.

The "outside" members of his team made sure that Scott accomplished his goal because he had made sure to show them that they were an important part of his team.

Honesty

Honesty means keeping the team informed on the current state of affairs of the company, and where they stand in relationship to it. An opportunity to display honesty may come up when confronting certain delicate situations, especially in the international arena, where bribery is not uncommon.

In working with international groups, we have been approached to compromise our integrity in order to facilitate transactions. It might be from the part of the buyer who asks for extra cash or goods that would help him make the decision to buy our product over the competitor's. There are very strong anti-bribery laws in place, and most companies have an anti-bribery policy.

But even without these laws, when confronted with bribery, a firm "NO" response, shows the members of the team the clear standards and principles that govern the group.

Positive outlook

 As mentioned before, I am a strong believer in influencing the energy around us. I know that if we give out positive energy, we will attract positive energy, this works in reverse also. There are many really interesting books written on this subject and most of us can relate to how this transfer of energy may have played a part in our own life. I do know that the team leader sets the energy meter for the whole group.

I refuse to allow members to say the word "problem." Once you grant permission to talk about problems, this seems to create a breeding ground for these little critters and soon one problem creates another and another until you find yourself buried in them.

What we call "problems" are often excuses for not accomplishing goals, or a reason to avoid responsibility. Every problem brings its own solution, and I'm always ready to listen to solutions. That is why in my teams we all have replaced the word "problem" with the word "opportunity." We look at road blocks or "bumps in the road" as "Opportunities to find a solution." These are opportunities to show that we can find another way, or an opportunity to learn how to adjust, and ultimately an opportunity to succeed no matter what comes along.

While working as the product manager of a company I experienced the negative impact that just hearing the word *"problem"* had on the members of the team. I was responsible for bringing new products to the market, as well as gathering feedback from the international sales group to report back to the engineering development staff.

The international sales group constantly reported *"problems"* with the various new products. When I passed these comments directly to the engineers these professionals went into a rage: "How can there be problems all the time with these people, they don't know anything!" Their attitude towards the international group grew more and more negative.

After evaluating the situation more closely, I realized that due to a lack in English language skills, the international people used the word "problem" when they meant to say that they had a *suggestion* or *question*. The word "problem" was the closest word they knew to express their concern, but it carried such negative energy that it adversely affected the relationship between groups.

Once I was able to identify that the word "problem" was the culprit, I promptly informed everyone in the international group to refrain from using that word and instead say *"I have a suggestion"* or "I *have a question about.*" What a difference that small change made! World War III was averted between the international sales group and the engineering group.

International teams are always faced with new challenging "opportunities:" These include fluctuating exchange rates, new economic issues, local elections, holidays, and an array of other reasons for why the sales can't be made.

But as we began to treat all of these as new "opportunities" to overcome obstacles, we actually found solutions. Even when working with customers in Venezuela, where economic and political complications have made it almost impossible for customers to obtain US dollars, we discovered ways to make some sales and get paid.

We are surrounded by examples of people that have taken an "opportunity" to overcome great odds to accomplish their goals. One of my favorite examples is the election of Barack Obama as president of the United States. He was able to reach the highest position in the world against the odds of prejudice.

No matter what anyone's political views or persuasions are, it is easy to recognize that Barak Obama had to clear unbelievably difficult obstacles to attain the most powerful post on the planet. Some of these obstacles included race, inexperience, youth, a difficult childhood, and a strange name. So you think you have "problems" that prevent you from reaching your goal? Think again.

Another example, very close to me is that of my friend Dr. Edmundo Muniz, a doctor from the Dominican Republic. He realized early in his career that he wanted to achieve much higher goals than he possibly could, if he stayed in his home country. He made the decision to travel to the United States, with his young family in tow, to pursue his dream of entering the University of Michigan epidemiology graduate program.

Some of his obstacles were, low finances, a language barrier, a family to feed, and, oh yes, entering the University of Michigan was a dream, but he had not been accepted yet, that was an additional obstacle.

Dr. Muniz approached each of these as "opportunities" to triumph over, and he cleared every one. He went on to pass the TOFEL (an English language proficiency exam) which he needed just to apply to the University.

In addition to a Masters in Science, he acquired a Ph.D. in Population Planning and International Health.

After his studies at the University of Michigan, he was accepted in the Epidemic Intelligence Service (EIS) program at the Centers for Disease Control and Prevention (CDC) where he became a disease and epidemic detective, in a program where only a small number of applicants are selected from hundreds of physicians and doctoral-level scientists who apply.

He has gone on hold other positions; such as Vice-President of Cancer Drug Development in a multinational pharmaceutical company and twice, including his current position, Chief Executive Officer of corporations.

There are never problems, but always "opportunities" to move forward, conquer and succeed.

Language barriers

One of the "opportunities" to avoid an obstacle (not a problem) in working with an international team is the language barrier. Most of my team members speak at

 least a basic level of English, but I still made it my responsibility to acquire a working knowledge of Spanish, French and Portuguese as needed.

However, that didn't end the misunderstandings that came with communicating in multiple languages, especially when none of them is your native tongue. But it did show deference and respect to the team members who spoke those languages.

Taking the extra time and effort, to speak slowly and enunciate clearly helps immensely to communicate plans, goals, and ideas to team members. Avoid using *slang*, *flowery* or particularly long words. Your team will appreciate it and be more impressed with you if you keep your vocabulary simple.

You will be surprised at how many ways there are to express what you want to say. My team members have repeatedly told me that they enjoy speaking in English with me because they can understand me when I speak, they also learn new words, according to them. Most of my team members prefer to speak English because they want to improve their skills, and sometimes, I am their English lesson for the day.

On one occasion I had the opportunity to bring two of my team members to the corporate office for some technical training. One was from Mexico and the other was from Brazil. In my introduction of the members to the person giving the training at corporate, I said, "this is Enrique, he is from Mexico and he speaks Spanish and pretty good English, and this is Pedro, he is from Brazil and he speaks excellent *Portuguese*." My point was that the trainer needed to speak slowly and clearly, to make sure that our international team members, who had limited English language skills, understood well the material that he was presenting. He needed to be patient, taking a bit more time to explain things and ask often if they understood.

Concept of time

This is an important issue when dealing with an international team. My mid-west upbringing taught me to value other people's time as I do my own. I plan things out and strive to meet deadlines. Whenever possible, I'm even early.

Time is a vague concept in some areas

of the world, Latin American being one of them, as the following experience in Peru taught me.

I went to make customer calls with one of my team members who informed me that our first meeting would be at 10am and that he would pick me up the hotel at 9am because we needed to drive a fair distance.

In my typical mid-west American fashion, I was waiting outside the hotel for my salesman at 8:45am. At 9:15am he still hadn't arrived, so I called him wanting to know if plans had changed. "No," he assured, me "I'm almost there." At 9:30am I called him again and he gave me the same answer. He finally showed up at 9:45am with a big smile and warm welcome.

I on the other hand, was starting my day with a big knot of frustration in my stomach over something that is quite important to me – punctuality.

My team member had an explanation of course, he said that he had gotten a late start that morning but that we would be okay with the customer. As it turned out we arrived at the customer's office at 11 am. Surprisingly, the customer didn't appear to be upset at all. So I dismissed the situation and figured things would be better the next day.

Actually the situation repeated itself the next morning. I again waited for my team member for 45 minutes. Once again we were late to meet the customer. This was not going to work for me.

I now take a very strong stand on being on time with my team. I express to them that time is a commodity that is not replaceable.

Our customers do appreciate that we show up when we say we will. In this area our group stands out by giving our customers something that others don't.

This is one instance where what may be culturally acceptable, can be improved on for the benefit of the business.

CHAPTER 5. – A RECAP

If you are a team leader of an international group, the following suggestions will assist you in achieving the desired success.

1. As the leader, you remain responsible for the outcome of your team, so it's important that you take strong ownership of the overall project. Always show your team that you are on the front line for them and demonstrate that you take your responsibilities seriously.

2. Have a clear understanding of the goals and objectives, so that you can communicate them to your team members in an unambiguous manner. Make sure that every team member understands clearly their role and obligations. Reiterate this regularly and often.

3. Realize that you cannot do everything by yourself, you need your team. Your team members are the body parts that will help move you forward, towards your goal.   Delegate responsibilities that your members can do well. Mentor them where needed but always stress that it is their responsibility to carry the tasks through.

4. Encourage the team to share their knowledge and information with each other so that the team can progress faster towards the goal.

5. Get to know the team members well enough so you can gain their trust, they will feel freer to provide input and express their true thoughts and ideas.

6. Provide useful tools for your team to do their jobs well.   Continually look for advancements in technology that will improve your team's performance.

7. Keep the energy level up by staying involved with your team and providing encouragement and praise for their contribution

8. Involve as many "outside" members as possible to be part of your team. They will assist the entire team in accomplishing their goals. Allow them to share in the glory of winning.

9. Turn every negative situation into an "opportunity" to grow, learn and succeed, and never let the word "problem" enter a conversation.

10. Share the glory of your successes with everyone in your team! And have fun!

I wish you all much success, and if you are interested in team building, remember that it really can become *"Stupid Simple"*.

Russ Steimle

https://www.linkedin.com/pub/russ-steimle/2/504/549

Because my team building abilities have been based on my life experiences, I cannot leave without acknowledging many of the people that have influenced me along the way.

So special thanks to:

Tina Muñiz-Steimle, My all-time greatest encourager, book editor, supporter and good sport to go along with my dreams.

Paul and Sylvia Steimle, My parents, true examples of strong work ethic, and the openers of the door to the wonderful world out there.

Bill Rhodes, My first boss and great team leader who taught me about empowerment and believed in me by giving me a chance to build on my strongest skills.

Joan Andrew, The Greatest boss I ever had, who by her example showed me how to stand up for the team, empower and encourage them.

Xavier Leroy, My French protégé, friend, brother, and "god-father" to my son, with his willingness to learn and grow was the reason that our French team functioned so well.

Pedro Gargalaca, My Brother, and believer in me, and encourager to write this book – I dedicate this book to you, Pedro.

Dr. Edmundo Muniz, My mentor and an example that there is always a way to overcome road blocks to move on to reach great successes.

Brian Levey, Thanks for giving me a chance to put my team building skills into practice, one more time.

Ricardo Lovetro, My Brazilian protégé and all around great team member that believes like I do, and will go on to become a great team leader also.

John Way, An example of a great "outside" team member, with his help and devotion to our team, our Brazil team was born.

Patrice Jaunasse, A great coach and mentor on goal planning, strategy building and demonstration of true meaning of transparency for the team and reminded me to keep a balance in niceness with the team members.

Rodrigo Puerta, An example that extreme high energy levels can come in a small package, and my reminder that basic communication requires emails to be answered in less than one minute and texts in less than 15 seconds.

Scott Reinginger, A great example of a praiser.

Also very important in my life:

Jennifer & Chris, Monica, Alexandru, Waldir, Ricardo G., Rafael, Mario, Edwardo, Krister, Milagros, Audrei, Luiz, Thiago, Augusto, Rene, Rita, Hugo, Sidnei, Marcia, Ricardo C., Alvaro, Guillermo, Salvador, Carlos and Carlos, Joham, Hector, Juan Esteban, Dania, Alejandro, Marcelo, Paulina, Phillip, Juan Carlos, Mayel, Steve, Eric M., Robert, Bernadette, Eric S., Fabrice, Annike, Olivier, Geoff, Nacho, Tim, Matthew, Gillian, Pietro, Marco, Andrea, Juan, Sergio, Gunter, Andreas, Norm, Jeff, Walter, Cheryl, Steve, Helmut, Keith, Norberto and the list could go on and on. Thank you all for being such an important part of my life.

Photo and clip art acknowledgement:

Cover photo: Andres Rodriguez Dreamstime.com
Inside vector images: Khoon Lay Gan 123RF.com
Michael Brown 123RF.com
Scusi 123RF.com
Huhulin 123RF.com

www.ingramcontent.com/pod-product-compliance
Lightning Source LLC
Chambersburg PA
CBHW070959180526
45168CB00003B/1219